He Likes All Of This

Daily Devotional For Women

By Chiquita N. Turner

Copyright © 2024 by Chiquita N. Turner

All rights reserved. No part of this book may be used or reproduced by any means, graphic, electronic, or mechanical, including photocopying, recording, taping, or by any information storage retrieval system, without the written permission of the publisher except in the case of brief quotations embodied in critical articles and reviews.

Contemporary English Version®
Copyright © 1995 American Bible Society. All rights reserved.

The ESV® Bible (The Holy Bible, English Standard Version®). ESV® Text Edition: 2016. Copyright © 2001 by Crossway, a publishing ministry of Good News Publishers. The ESV® text has been reproduced in cooperation with and by permission of Good News Publishers. Unauthorized reproduction of this publication is prohibited. All rights reserved.

Scriptures marked KJV are taken from the KING JAMES VERSION (KJV): KING JAMES VERSION, public domain.

THE HOLY BIBLE, NEW INTERNATIONAL VERSION®, NIV®
Copyright © 1973, 1978, 1984, 2011 by Biblica, Inc.® Used by permission. All rights reserved worldwide.

Scripture quotations marked NLT are taken from the *Holy Bible*, New Living Translation, copyright © 1996, 2004, 2015 by Tyndale House Foundation. Used by permission of Tyndale House Publishers, Inc., Carol Stream, Illinois 60188. All rights reserved.

New American Standard Bible®, Copyright © 1960, 1971, 1977, 1995, 2020 by The Lockman Foundation. All rights reserved.

Contents

Introduction 1

Dedication 4

Day 1: He Likes Your Smile 5

Day 2: He Likes Your Personality 7

Day 3: He Likes to be Acknowledged 9

Day 4: He Likes my Attitude 11

Day 5: He Likes to be Touched 15

Day 6: House of Peace & Rest 17

Day 7: You are a Great Mother 19

Day 8: He Likes my Confidence 21

Day 9: Take Pleasure in Cooking for Your Husband 23

Day 10: Sassy & Classy 25

Day 11: He Likes Your Body 29

Day 12: He Likes to be Teased 31

Day 13: Respect is What he Needs 35

Day 14: He Likes Humility 37

Day 15: I Know his Love Language 39

Day 16: He Likes When I Pray for Him 43

Day 17: Don't Judge Him 45

Day 18: He Likes That I'm his Safe Place 47

Day 19: Communication is Everything 51

Day 20: Unity: Us Against the World 53

Day 21: Your Enemy is the Devil, not Your Husband 55

Day 22: Wife to Wife 59

Special Acknowledgements 61

Journal Pages 63

Chiquita N. Turner

Introduction

I'm excited to share this daily motivational with you, this book is designed to empower and encourage you to be the best wife you can be for your husband. As we know marriage isn't an easy task but it's a daily task that takes a lot of work. Marriage isn't already made perfect, but it can be made better once you understand that your spouse isn't perfect. Perfect people don't make a good marriage, but imperfect people that's determine to love and work through every difficult moment make a good marriage.

You should feel good every day to wake up knowing you were chosen to be his wife and chosen to empower and encourage him to be the best man he can be for himself, for God and his family. His thrive and strive is dependent upon what he is being fed at home. I'm not talking about food, but I'm talking about your energy and your words you use towards your husband. As a wife we must understand we have power to break him or build him.

Live everyday building your man up, I know he might get on your nerves, and it might even be seen as you are doing all the work but if you remain consistent, you will soon see a boomerang effect. I want you to know this, your husband really does love you. Be patient with him and he will prove it to you sooner than you think. Remain faithful, respectful and make every day lovely by speaking positivity to your husband. Let this book guide you into your deeper perspective of your marriage, once your perspective changes you will see the good and the love your husband truly has inside him.

Let me encourage you to be a wise wife not a foolish wife. Remember he chose you because he likes everything about you, who you are, what you bring to his life, and how you make him feel as a man. Yep, he likes all of that. Don't be quick to throw him away, don't be quick to give up on him, and don't be quick to ignore him, but be wise and pray for him daily. I pray this all time for myself, Lord, help me to humble and sweet, lowly and meek. Meaning Lord help me to stay humble, not quick to judge, or jump to conclusions but help me to stay low in my attitude and keep me sweet, I don't want to be bitter. I want to be a blessing to my husband.

Bless your husband today with your kind words and smile. Only speak encouragement and pray for the things that bothers you about your spouse. Know that God will hear your cry and your prayers, so tell him all about it. Watch God work out your concerns. So, smile, you have your husband's heart, and he trusts you with it.

"He Likes All of This" was born out of a very difficult time in my marriage. I actual begin writing this book in 2021. This unfortunate event left me feeling unwanted and inadequate. I remember thinking "Is something wrong with me", but deep down, I knew the kind of woman I am. Despite this, Satan tried to convince me that I wasn't enough for my husband, making me feel terrible about myself.

Thank God for the power of prayer. God immediately spoke to me, reminding me that I am enough. He began to reveal all the things my husband liked about me, listing each one and reaffirming my worth. The devil is a liar—don't believe his lies. You are enough, and the truth is, your husband likes all of it.

Love is a powerful action that compels you to let go of anger, bitterness, and resentment. Instead, we learned to forgive, communicate more and seek solutions instead of staying mad. Marriage counseling also helped us. Allow God to work in your marriage and fight for you. You are beautifully and wonderfully made by Him, and everything God made is good. You are enough!

Heavenly Father, encourage every wife or woman who reads this book. Allow her to feel your peace and presence on every page she reads. Open her eyes to see a different perspective as she views her marriage. Help her to see you in her husband. Renew, Refresh, and Rebuild every marriage In Jesus' name, Amen!

1 Corinthians 13:4-8 NIV

Love is patient, love is kind. It does not envy, it does not boast, it is not proud. It does not dishonor others, it is not self-seeking, it is not easily angered, and it keeps no record of wrongs. Love does not delight in evil but rejoices with the truth. It always protects, always trusts, always hopes, and always perseveres. Love never fails.

1 Peter 4:8 NIV

Above all, love each other deeply, because love covers over a multitude of sins.

Dedication

I would like to dedicate this book to every wife and woman. You are enough!

Chiquita N. Turner

DAY 1 He Likes Your Smile

Believe it or not, your husband loves to see you smile. Your smile was probably one of the first things he noticed about you. When you smile, it brightens everything around him, dispelling any darkness. There is immense power in your smile; it signals happiness and warmth. This means your husband doesn't have to wonder if today is a good day for you or not. It gives him a clear sign that his wife is in a good mood. Every husband loves to see his wife happy. You've heard the saying, "Happy wife, happy life," right? While every day may not be filled with sunshine, be intentional and keep smiling no matter what.

Choosing to smile is a powerful decision. Make smiling your choice today. It's easy to hold onto things that make you sad, but remember, your husband doesn't want you to be sad. Don't let small things stop you from loving on your husband today. He needs your smile, and you need to feel his love. Smile today and every day so your husband can feel comfortable being around you and free to be himself. When you smile, it's like the "open" sign outside your favorite store—when that sign is lit up, you smile and go right in, right? The same concept applies to your marriage. Your smile brings joy to your home; a happy wife creates a happy life.

So today, be intentional. Smile more and treat yourself to some new lip glosses and shades of lipsticks. Shine and smile more, your man is looking forward to your smile today. Smile; someone is thinking about you.

Heavenly Father, thank you for your goodness and kindness towards us. Help me to continue to smile in the good times and the bad times, knowing you are able to fix everything that's wrong. Help me to be the wife my husband needs. In Jesus' name, Amen!

Proverbs 15:13 NASB

A joyful heart makes a cheerful face, But when the heart is sad, the spirit is broken

DAY 2 He Likes Your Personality

Personality is everything for a man, which is why you are his wife. Your personality was like no other. Whether you are bubbly, funny, confident, friendly, ambitious, adventurous, energetic, humble, charismatic, or optimistic, your personality drew him to you. He felt good being around you and with you. Your husband loves everything about you. Your personality brings out the best in him.

That's why it's crucial for you to stay true to yourself and not transform into someone completely different. Such a drastic change can lead to unhappiness in your marriage. This works both ways—you know how you would feel if your husband completely changed his personality. You wouldn't like the new person because you fell in love with your spouse's original personality, which is what attracts you to him.

Many times, in marriages, we change on our spouse, and we wonder why things don't feel the same and why our spouse isn't into us like they once were. It's because something happened along the way in our personality. You changed how you were, and now you are this new person that he doesn't recognize and isn't drawn to. Don't allow circumstances, life battles, or even challenges in your marriage to change your personality. You must remember that your husband's personality draws you, and your personality draws him. Change for the better, not for the worse.

You have the tools to make things better in your marriage. Don't stop doing the things that he's drawn to. Don't stop giving him what he's looking for from you. Don't stop being his woman, his girlfriend, his bae, his boo. Your man loves all that about you, and only you know what that is. He's your husband; please him by being the best you. As you grow together, you will learn new things about your husband, so pay attention. Age will definitely bring about a change, but even with aging, change for the better, not worse. Be attentive to each other's needs; don't ignore each other's desires and irritations. Remember, he likes you, so you are the one he needs in his life.

So today, examine yourself. Check your attitude and your actions. Make sure you haven't changed who you are. Make sure you're not withholding anything from your husband. Be that sweet, loving, attractive woman he fell in love with. Be the best you!

Heavenly Father, thank you for making us better for each other. Help us to be attentive to each other's needs and desires. Help us to change for the better, help us to remain focused on loving each other. In Jesus' name, Amen!

Luke 6:31 NIV

Do to others as you would have them do to you.

DAY 3 He Likes to be Acknowledged

The truth is, every man likes to be acknowledged, and he should be acknowledged by you. If you are looking for ways to build your husband up, this is an effective way to do so. Acknowledging your man both in his presence and absence speaks volumes to his headship and ego. Yes, we know ego plays a part in acknowledgment, but as wives, we don't mind pumping up his ego. Right? Acknowledging your husband's presence when he enters a room makes him feel appreciated. Appreciation is the motor that drives your husband to do more for you. It's the fuel that makes him go harder for you every day.

When you don't acknowledge his presence, it's a sign of disrespect. The main thing a husband needs from his wife is respect. You should be glad to see your man walk through those doors. Get up, get off the phone, stop what you are doing, and speak to your husband. Acknowledge his presence in the room. I've learned that my husband likes to hear me say, "I've got to go, my honey just walked in the house." This makes him feel important and appreciated. He's your man, so make sure you make him feel like the man of the house by acknowledging him. Teach your children to acknowledge him by speaking to him when he comes into the house and not ignoring his presence.

This is another tool you can use to build up your husband. He likes all of this. If you want to keep your man encouraged, keep building him up with acknowledgments and appreciation.

Acknowledge his efforts, let him know you noticed he finished the yard work, or whatever the task is. Acknowledge the things he does right, and the things he attempts to do (but encourage him to finish). Acknowledge and celebrate his accomplishments. This pushes him to do even more and to finish more assignments and tasks.

So today, when your husband walks through those doors, don't forget your smile, but also acknowledge his presence and let him know how happy you are to see him. Stroke your man's ego and tell him how things are better now that he's home. Your husband loves this about you, so don't allow anything or anyone to keep you from acknowledging your man, no matter where you are. It speaks volumes in your marriage.

Heavenly Father, help us today to acknowledge our husbands. Help us to remember to address him when he comes into the room, or wherever we might be. Help us to remember to celebrate his accomplishments and his willingness or attempts to finish tasks. Teach us how to show him we really do appreciate him for all he does for us and his family. In Jesus' name, Amen!

Romans 12:10 NIV

Be devoted to one another in love. Honor one another above yourselves.

DAY 4 He Likes my Attitude

A woman with a good attitude will capture any man's attention. If you asked your husband what caught his attention about you, he will most likely mention your attitude along with other attributes he noticed. I remember when I asked my husband this question, he first mentioned my physical appearance (of course—that's a man for you). However, he also said it was my attitude. He loves that I have a good attitude. I wasn't stuck up, snobby, or moody, but had a pleasant demeanor.

Your attitude is everything. Let's be honest—you are not drawn to people with bad attitudes; it's not attractive. Your husband loves that he has a wife who is not uptight, mean, selfish, or self-centered. He loves that you are down to earth, sweet, caring, loving, sensitive, considerate, and concerned. What a woman—he loves this about you.

There are many successful women who has bad attitudes. She might be attractive and successful, but if she has a bad attitude, a man won't be interested in her. It's surprising to hear this because you might think that a woman who fits his physical preferences—big legs, big breasts, big butt, slim waist—would be exactly what he wants. Not so. It's her attitude that truly attracts men.

I'm not implying that women with big legs, big breasts, and big butts have bad attitudes. What I mean is that being physically attractive isn't the most important factor in a man's eyes. It's the attitude a woman carries that truly captures a man's attention. Case in point: Have you ever seen a handsome, successful man with a woman you might consider unattractive? I certainly have. You come across such couples and wonder how she ended up with him. What does he see in her? You might perceive her as unattractive, and you ponder how this relationship happened, why he chose someone like her. The answer is clear: it was her attitude. It was the way she made that man feel about himself. It was her smile, her personality. It's not always about outer appearance. That woman simply has a great attitude, and that handsome man was drawn to her because of it.

Vice versa have you ever seen an unattractive man with a very attractive wife? I have, and you wonder how he got her. I bet you're thinking of a couple right now. It's not about appearance; that man's good attitude and the way he cared for her won her over. Being attractive means nothing to a woman if you have a bad attitude.

Your husband loves your pleasant attitude. Have you noticed when you have a bad attitude, your husband really can't handle it? It makes him pull away a little, you know why? He's not drawn to it; he's driven away. That's why it's crucial not to hold onto this kind of attitude for too long. You don't want to push your husband away; you want to attract him to you every day. So, don't cling to a bad or nasty attitude. Let it go! Stay pleasant, sweet, and loving so your husband looks forward to coming home to you every day.

So today, wear your good attitude, smile, something good will happen for you today!

Heavenly Father, help us as wives keep a positive and a good attitude towards our husbands. Help us to forgive him for the things he might have done or even said that would cause us to have a bad attitude. Continue to teach us how to draw him and not drive him. In Jesus' name, Amen!

Ephesians 4:31-32 KJV

Let all bitterness, and wrath, and anger, and clamor, and evil speaking, be put away from you, with all malice: And be ye kind one to another, tenderhearted, forgiving one another, even as God for Christ's sake hath forgiven.

He Likes All Of This

DAY 5 He Likes to be Touched

There's something magical about a woman's touch that makes everything better. It's one of the special gifts God gave us. Touching soothes and calms; it's powerful. Your husband loves it when you touch him. He enjoys feeling your soft hands warmly embracing him, especially after a long day of work, after tough meetings, after a rough day, or even on a good day. When your hands rub against his face, head, back, arms, and hands, he feels better. Your touch melts away his doubts, stress, and worries.

Your husband loves to be touched. Touching your husband while talking to him relaxes him. If you want your man to relax, chill out, and not be frustrated, tense, when communicating with you, try touching him while you talk. Notice how his entire attitude changes. This isn't about touching him in a sexual way; it goes deeper than that. Embrace your husband's body in ways that provide him with security and relief.

Your husband needs to feel your hands on him. Make it a daily habit to rub him, even if you are just sitting and watching TV. Use your special gift, your soft hands. Massage your husband's head, the back of his neck, his muscles, his arms, and his shoulders. Help your husband relax and find relief. Don't stop touching, even when you're in the car together. Your touch improves his life. Hold his hand; it shows him you're with him no matter what. Your touch conveys a powerful message all on its own.

A marriage without touching is a thirsty marriage; it's drying up! Can you imagine how your husband would feel if you never touched him? Your spouse needs to be embraced by the one who loves him the most. Your touch reminds him of the unconditional love you have for him. Your touch eases his insecurities and brings assurance to his heart that everything will be alright. No matter how others treat him throughout the day, his wife will make it better when he gets home. When was the last time you touched your husband? Again, not in a sexual way. If you can't remember, it's been too long. Use your special gift; it's uplifting and comforting. Most women understand how powerful touching is, which is why we are mindful when other women touch while talking to our husbands, knowing the messages touch can convey.

Keep touching him; in fact, increase your touching. When you walk by him, put your hands on him. Send your message to him through your touch today, letting him know, "I see you; I got you. I am your rest; I am your peace." Your husband loves to be touched by you. So, tonight when you get into bed, touch him. Put him to sleep, as you touch, pray for him!

Heavenly Father, thank you for giving me this special weapon touching. Thank you for teaching me how to embrace, how to calm and relax my husband. Thank you for using my hands to bring him comfort. Continue to show me ways to help my husband relieve all concerns. In Jesus' name, Amen!

Matthew 18:19 KJV

"Again I say unto you, that if two of you shall agree on earth as touching anything that they shall ask, it shall be done for them of my Father which is in heaven."

DAY 6 House of Peace & Rest

Your husband finds refuge in your home. He loves the way you manage and maintain it, relieving him of any worries about its upkeep. From cleaning to handling daily tasks, you keep everything running smoothly. Even if he hasn't explicitly expressed his appreciation, trust that he truly values it. You make him feel like a king by caring for your home and creating a peaceful environment. The way you organize each room and add those special touches to make it beautiful. he loves all it.

Men might not often mention it, but they do notice how you care for the home and your daily routines. Whether it's making the bed every morning, lighting candles, or ensuring the kitchen is clean each night, he sees the importance you place on these habits. Sometimes, he even adopts these routines himself because he understands how crucial they are to maintaining the household.

It's wonderful to walk into a clean, good-smelling room after a long day. Our happy place is our home, and we feel good when everything is in place and the house is fresh. It relaxes us and says, "Welcome home." Because I love this welcoming feeling, I'm always looking for things that bring joy, light, and peace to our home. Remember, your home should be his place of rest and peace. Keep the atmosphere peaceful!

Safeguard the peace that resides in your home; it's not just a place for your husband to rest but for you and your children as well.

Whether you live in an apartment or a house, peace is a gift from God that allows us to live comfortably in this world. Amidst a chaotic and often evil world, you need a sanctuary where the entire family can find tranquility. When your home creates this atmosphere, you are cultivating peacemakers within your household. It teaches positivity, calmness, and promotes healthy attributes in everyone. Be intentional about creating this kind of environment so that your mind, body, and soul can rest peacefully.

Today, find ways to refresh your home with new decor, candles, or a fresh coat of paint. Feel free to switch things up, whether it's rearranging the furniture or opening the blinds to let in natural sunlight. These are just suggestions that I enjoy for our home, but you can choose what works best for you. A home filled with peace is a place where your husband will always want to be. Create an environment that makes it hard for him to stay away, with your positive attitude and a serene atmosphere. Your home is his sanctuary, and your bed is his place of rest. Keep your sheets clean and hot ready for whatever he desires.

Heavenly Father, thank you for teaching me how to care for our home, thank you for helping me make our home a place of peace, love, and comfort. Thank you for giving me creative ways to enhance our home. Thank you for bringing my husband home every day safely. In Jesus' name, Amen!

2 Thessalonians 3:16 NIV

"Now may the Lord of peace himself give you peace at all times and in every way. The Lord be with all of you.

Chiquita N. Turner

DAY 7 You are a Great Mother

Momma knows best, and your husband already sees this! The way you care for the children reflects your deep love for them. He loves how you dedicate time to his children and ensure that both the house and the kids are well looked after. He never has to worry about their needs because you're such a good wife. Just as you take care of him, he knows you will take care of the children as well. It's a wonderful feeling for him to know that his children have the best mother ever. He might not always say it, but he truly appreciates everything you do for them.

You're an incredible mom, and your husband deeply values how balanced you are in managing so much daily. That's why he loves you so much. You handle things he could never do. You juggle numerous tasks simultaneously: you work, maintain a clean home, cook, and take care of the children. You wash and fold clothes, organize closets and drawers, teach and help with schoolwork and projects, and run from practices to games. You are amazing! You rock!

The World's Greatest Mom award goes to you. I celebrate you today. It's not always easy, but it's something we have to do as moms. You are the glue that holds your family together; you are the propeller that keeps the ship moving. I know it can get frustrating at times, but steal away and take a moment for yourself, exhale, and jump back in there. You've got this. Find joy in caring for your children. Your children will grow up and thank you for all your hard work. Your husband might not say thank you all the time, but your children will one day appreciation you. Because you are the Best Mom Ever!

Heavenly Father, thank you for blessing me with children. I know children are a blessing from you. Help and strengthen me to continue to teach and train them. Cover my children in your blood, give them a sweet and obedient spirit. Help them to be best they can be. Help them every day to complete tasks and assignments. In Jesus' name, Amen!

Proverbs 31: 28-29 ESV

Her children rise up and call her blessed; her husband also, and he praises her: "Many women have done excellently, but you surpass them all."

DAY 8 He Likes my Confidence

There's nothing that compares to a confident woman. A confident woman is someone who accomplishes everything she sets her mind to. She's unstoppable. Your husband loves your confidence. You are self-driven and self-motivated to achieve your personal and family goals. Confidence looks good on you. You are a strong woman who moves to your own beat. When others doubt you, you always prove them wrong because you know who you are and believe that if you want it, you can have it. Nothing is impossible for you.

You have confidence not only in yourself but also in your husband. Trust his decisions, believe in his plans, and encourage him to be the best man he can be. Motivate him with your kind words, empower him with your prayers, and push him by reminding him that he's capable. Don't lose confidence in your husband. Even if he doesn't plan, organize, or balance life like you do, don't discourage him. Instead, encourage him by letting him know you trust he'll handle the situation.

Sometimes it's challenging when you see a better way to handle a situation, but it's important to let him lead and trust that he knows what's best for the family. Your confidence in him means the world to him. When you believe in him and trust him, he will work hard to prove that he's got it. Affirm to him that you trust his judgment and believe he knows what's best for the family, and then step back. Your confidence in him is exactly what he needs.

Heavenly Father, Thank you for another day. Thank you for teaching me to have confidence in my husband and his guidance for our family. Continue to give my husband wisdom to make the right decisions concerning our family. In Jesus' name, Amen!

Hebrews 10:35 NIV

So do not throw away your confidence; it will be richly rewarded.

Chiquita N. Turner

DAY 9 Take Pleasure in Cooking for Your Husband

The kitchen holds a special place in your home; it's where love is prepared for the entire family through meals. Cooking should bring joy, as it allows you to nourish your husband with meals that satisfy his physical needs. It's an intimate space where the family gathers to share the cares of their day and discuss plans for the future. Cooking for your husband is not just about food; it's also about connecting with him, understanding his day, and his thoughts. Creating meals that your family enjoys sets a wonderful atmosphere for spending quality time together.

In the hustle and bustle of our busy lives, finding time to cook a meal for your man can sometimes feel like an impossible task. But fear not, takeout is always an option! Whether you whip up something homemade or order for takeout, the key is being intentional about sitting down together for dinner. Even when your schedules clash and time seems to slip away, make it a priority to schedule out moments to share a meal. These moments of togetherness are essential for the health of your marriage. Bonding during mealtime goes beyond just filling your stomachs; it strengthens your connection, improves communication, and deepens intimacy.

In the midst of our chaotic lives, these small moments of connection become precious gems. They create lasting memories and bonds that withstand the test of time. So, seize every opportunity to get to know your husband better, to laugh together, to share stories, and to simply enjoy each other's company. These moments will be the ones you cherish forever.

Establishing mealtime traditions is a cornerstone of family culture. It sets the stage for unforgettable moments and creates a legacy for your children to carry into their own lives. Through family recipes passed down through generations, you're not just sharing food; you're sharing stories, values, and love. These moments weave the fabric of your family's identity and create bonds that endure through life's ups and downs.

So, embrace the opportunity to cook for your family, knowing that each meal is a chance to create memories, strengthen bonds, and foster a sense of belonging that lasts a lifetime.

Heavenly Father, I thank you for my family and thank you for giving us our daily bread. It is you that has provided for us. When I am tired and overwhelmed give me strength to make memories and prepare meals for my family. In Jesus' name, Amen!

1 Peter 3:1 ESV

Likewise, wives, be subject to your own husbands, so that even if some do not obey the word, they may be won without a word by the conduct of their wives,

DAY 10 Sassy & Classy

You're such a lady, and your husband loves the way you carry yourself both in public and at home. Your boldness and impeccable demeanor shine everywhere you go. Your confidence in speaking out for yourself and others impresses your man. He feels proud knowing he has a woman who handles herself with grace and still knows how to be humble enough to let her man lead. Sassy and classy, you embody a woman who knows her worth.

This kind of woman prepares for her day with both her appearance and a mindset ready to tackle responsibilities at home and in the workplace. She is a leader, often recognized as a woman of high quality. Her actions and leadership are impeccable, always showing respect to others. Her man loves this about her; he's never intimidated by her elegance and leadership style. She avoids gossip and negativity, focusing on improving things for her household.

Her conversations with others are straightforward, and she's honest with everyone. This kind of woman knows how to control her emotions and actions in difficult situations. She can gracefully respond to insults and will always defends her family. She's smart, funny, and beautiful, and your man loves all these qualities in you. Don't be afraid to let this side of you shine through. Often, we shy away from the sassy part because of insecurities or fear. It's okay to be bold, outgoing, and, most importantly, yourself.

He Likes All Of This

This kind of woman knows how to drive her man crazy, she confidently flaunts herself around him, even if she doesn't feel at her most attractive. Your man loves all of it. It's not always about physical appearance; it's about having the confidence that your man appreciates everything about you. You're not too much for him—you're just right. A confident woman knows how to captivate her man with her words, spunk and passionate edge. Don't let insecurities hold you back from pleasing your man. You don't have to look perfect—but put on your best dress or your best lingerie and snatch his attention when you walk in. A sassy woman walks with authority and gets what she wants. Embrace your confidence and let it shine.

Your sassiness and classiness make you incredibly sexy and irresistible to your husband. Relax, he's your man. Be comfortable in your own body, regardless of size or shape, and embrace your flaws. Share everything with him—he will cherish it all. You were made for him, and it's your heart he loves the most. Among all your wonderful qualities, your heart is the most beautiful part.

So today, unleash your sassiness and shake your man to his core. Be strong and stay confident.

Heavenly Father, help us not to lose the fire we once had for our husbands. Give us that love back, that excitement back for our husbands. Renew our affection for one another. Help us to continue to love on each other as husband and wife. In Jesus' name, Amen!

1 Corinthians 7:3-4 NIV

"The husband should fulfill his marital duty to his wife, and likewise the wife to her husband. The wife does not have authority

over her own body but yields it to her husband. In the same way, the husband does not have authority over his own body but yields it to his wife."

He Likes All Of This

DAY 11 He Likes Your Body

Let's talk about it! Your body! Many women are unhappy with their body image; over 90% of women struggle with their appearance, according to Google. As women, we must stop comparing our bodies to the artificially enhanced images we see in the media and on social media. The truth is your husband noticed something sexy about you. Whether it was your lips, breasts, butt, legs, or hips, something caught his attention. Men are visual beings; and while every man is different, your husband chose you because he liked what he saw. He noticed your smile, but your body more than likely got his attention first. He saw your imperfections and was still attracted to you. So don't be hard on yourself. If your man likes it, flaunt it!

Some of us have been through a lot—having babies, facing health challenges, dealing with stress and depression—that has caused weight gain or weight loss. I want to encourage you to embrace your scars, stretch marks, and cellulite. Your husband loves you and doesn't care about those things when you take your clothes off. He likes all of that. Remain confident that you have everything your man needs. Be free and confident; your spunk will light his match.

Your body is what your husband needs, so never withhold it from him. I know our lives are busy, and we have a lot on our plates. You might not feel like being intimate every night but pray and ask God to help you to satisfy your husband's needs and desires. Your husband not only likes your body, but he also needs it.

Your body has the ability to relieve his stress and frustrations. Your body cultivates, stimulates, and deepens his connection with you. If you desire more connection, have more sex and communication. Verbal expressions produce closeness, acceptance, validation, and excitement. If he doesn't know what you like, tell him. Speak up; your man desires emotional intimacy with you. Don't starve your man; overfeed him.

So today, do something spontaneous for your husband, something unexpected. Drain him until he can't take any more. Give him what he wants—your body!

Heavenly Father, thank you for helping me when I felt unattractive. Help me to embrace my body that you have given to me. Help me during the times when I don't feel like being intimate with my husband, give me strength and excitement to satisfy his desires. Deepen our connection spiritually and emotionally. In Jesus' name, Amen!

Psalm 139:13-14 ESV

For you formed my inward parts; you knitted me together in my mother's womb. I praise you, for I am fearfully and wonderfully made. Wonderful are your works; my soul knows it very well

DAY 12 He Likes to be Teased

When was the last time you had some fun with your husband? I'm not talking about game night or a joke here and there. I mean, when was the last time you set the tone for an explosive night? Do you still flirt with your husband? I hope you do. That's your man, and you know what he likes. He likes to be teased. Wives don't lose your mojo or your ability to make your man go crazy before he even sees you. This is very important to keep alive in your marriage. You still got it, so use it! I know most of the time we wait for him to set the tone and pursue us but relax and have fun throughout the day with your husband. Remember, he's your man.

Believe me when I say, he loves for you to tease him. Send a text message throughout the day with something like, "I know you're probably busy, but I want you to know I'm thinking about what I'm going to do to you when you get home." That man might be busy at work, but that message is going to send fire through him! He will definitely hurry his workday up. I'm sure he's going to text you back quickly with something like, "Tell me what you're thinking about doing." I'm telling you he like to be teased. There's so much you can do throughout the day to tease your man and make his day better. Tell him how much you want him and need him. Hearing your affirmations boosts his confidence.

You still got it, so bring the excitement back into your marriage. Have fun with your husband, live, laugh, and have lots of sex. Yep,

He Likes All Of This

I said it. That's your man. Leave a pair of your thongs or sexy underwear on the dashboard of his car. Think of creative ways to make your husband hurry back home. Write a short, detailed note about what you want to do to him and place it in his wallet. There are so many ways to tease your husband. I believe the reason why so many marriages are failing is that they have lost the fire they once had for one another.

Switch it up and remember how you were when you were dating. You put a lot of thought into your appearance, make sure you look and smell good. Yes, many of us are sanctified women, but listen to me closely: when it comes to this part of your marriage, you are free to do whatever is pleasing to your husband. Your husband does not need his sanctified wife on a date; he needs his fun spontaneous woman. There's a time and place for everything, and date night, kick-it night, or fun night is NOT the time for you to be sanctimonious. Be satisfying!

Date often, plan ahead for it, set the tone for the entire day, and be creative and intentional with your outfit, the car ride, the dinner, and even when you get home. It's okay to listen to love songs as part of setting the tone and the tease. You know what songs to play. The car ride is the most intense moment while on a date. Keep it spicy. Earlier in my book, I talked about non-sexual touching, but in this chapter, while on this date with your husband, all touching is sexual. Slow him down; he might try to rush the night. So don't forget to use your secret weapon: touching he loves when you tease him, so don't stop doing it. Keep the fire going and hot in your marriage. The more touching, the more time spent with each other, and the more intimacy you have with each other, the less room you leave for the devil. Keep it spicy!!

Heavenly Father, thank you for my husband. We have had some difficult times, and I'm sure we will have more in the future but help us to remember and consider each other daily. Help us to make time to date and to cherish every moment together. Help us to come out of complacency and to draw on our creativity when it comes to our relationship, even in our intimate moments. Thank you for renewing us and our affection. In Jesus' name, Amen!

Ecclesiastes 3:1 NIV

"There is a time for everything"

He Likes All Of This

DAY 13 Respect is What he Needs

Here's the secret to your husband's heart: RESPECT! All he needs is respect from you. Think about it; it's not much to ask for, right? Sometimes we think loving our husband is all he needs, but it's not. He needs to feel respected. The effect of not showing him respect triggers resentment. It makes him feel unappreciated and less masculine. Sometimes, as women, we can be unintentionally disrespectful with our tone and forceful attitudes. When your husband feels respected, he will give you the world. A respected man works extra hard to make sure you don't want for anything.

Respect for a man is like feeling loved for a woman; it's something they deeply need. When we don't feel loved, we feel sad and unwanted. Sometimes, we get it twisted, thinking our husbands just need our love, but respect is crucial for them. This is the key to his heart. When you treat your man with respect, he will open up more to you and begin to understand your needs. A respected man expresses his love for you in a much greater way. You will feel the love you've always longed for from your husband. It's a win-win relationship: you give him respect, and he gives you love.

Respect empowers him to be the best version of himself, embrace being respectful this will create beautiful love and balance in your marriage. The main goal is for both partners equally get what they need in the relationship. These efforts create harmony, appreciation, love, deeper connection, valued and cherished. Respect is what he needs from you!

So today, make respect a priority in your marriage and embrace the love he gives you in return. Watch God transform your marriage when both partners show equal dedication.

Heavenly Father, help us to show our husband's respect. Even during difficult times, help us to remember to always honor them and show them how much we care. Teach us how to talk to them and how to respond. We desire to be pleasing to our husbands, not hurtful. In Jesus' name, Amen!

1 Peter 3:8 NIV

Finally, all of you, be like-minded, be sympathetic, love one another, be compassionate and humble.

DAY 14 He Likes Humility

Humility isn't a weakness, ladies. It's a powerful expression of love and respect for your husband. Being humble means, you care so much for your partner that you're willing to change your approach and perspective to make him feel valued and empowered. Our goal should be to ensure he always feels like the head of the family. Let him lead and be ready to support and assist him in any endeavor or plan he might have.

Humility is the new sexy. Being humble, sweet, and gentle is the way to be. Try it, and watch your husband love you even more. It's okay to take the low role; humility is a beautiful posture. It allows you to see your spouse more clearly and serve your family with a willing heart. A humble woman finds joy in submitting to her man, especially when he loves and honors her. Even strong, independent women can easily submit to a strong leader when he knows how to guide correctly.

Humility is the new sexy. The truth is women often appreciate when their husbands take charge and lead. When a husband understands and embraces his role as the leader, the wife's heart naturally humbles. Your man likes to be the man of the house; let him be the leader God created him to be. Remember, you're his wife, his helper, and his supporter. Don't get ahead of him and try to lead. Instead, stand beside him, encouraging him to lead.

So today, how can you show humility? Step back and let him lead the family. Show support for whatever decision he makes.

Heavenly Father, help us embrace humility and show respect to our husbands. Teach us to support and encourage them as they lead our families. Help us to be humble, gentle, and loving. In Jesus' name, Amen!

Philippines 2:3-4 ESV

Do nothing from selfish ambition or conceit, but in humility count others more significant than yourselves. Let each of you look not only to his own interests, but also to the interests of others.

Chiquita N. Turner

DAY 15 I know his Love Language

Do you know your husband's love language? If you don't, take the time to find out. Observe him, ask him, and discover what truly makes him feel loved and appreciated. I encourage you to look up the five love languages you might be surprised by what your husband's love language is (Words of Affirmation, Acts of Service, Receiving of Gifts, Quality Time, and Physical Touch.) I wish I had known this earlier in our marriage; it would have saved us from countless arguments and frustrations. Understanding your spouse's love language can transform your relationship.

Have you ever wondered why your spouse seems unhappy, or why nothing you do seems to satisfy them? Why they always find something wrong with your gestures or acts of kindness? It's because you may not know their love language, or you might be ignoring it and giving them what you want them to have, not what they truly need.

We had it all backwards! My husband was expressing love in his love language, while I was showing mine. This mismatch left us frustrated and unfulfilled because we weren't meeting each other's needs. Despite our good intentions, we miscommunicated simply because we didn't understand each other's love language. Some might think this isn't important, but I'm here to tell you that it is crucial for a flourishing marriage. Knowing your spouse's love language helps you communicate better and provide what they truly desire.

He Likes All Of This

Using your spouse's love language daily will strengthen your marriage. Understanding how to show love in their language will, in return, make your spouse feel more appreciated. If your marriage needs improvement and a deeper connection, start by learning and discovering their love language. This simple step can resolve many issues you might be facing. Don't overlook the importance of knowing how your spouse receives love. Every person is different, and every relationship is unique. You can't give your spouse what you think they need; you must learn what makes them happy and how they like to receive love. Remember, every man isn't the same, and every woman isn't the same. Learn your partner, and watch how it will strengthen your communication, prevent problems, increase intimacy, and deepen your connection.

So today, identify and understand your husband's love language and start operating in it. Give him what he truly desires from you. If he doesn't know yours, communicate it to him so he can start giving you what you need. It's that simple! Trust me, you both will be happier.

Heavenly Father, thank you for giving me understanding to hear my husband's heart when he speaks, and thank you for making us all unique and different, show me how to properly minister to my husband. In Jesus' name, Amen!

1 Corinthians 13: 4-8 NIV

Love is patient, love is kind. It does not envy, it does not boast, it is not proud. It does not dishonor others, it is not self-seeking, it is not easily angered, it keeps no record of wrongs. Love does not delight in evil but rejoices with the truth. It always protects, always trusts, always hopes, and always perseveres. Love never fails. But where there are prophecies, they will cease; where there are tongues, they will be stilled; where there is knowledge, it will pass away.

He Likes All Of This

Chiquita N. Turner

DAY 16 He Likes When I Pray for Him

Your husband needs your prayers every day! A wise woman understands the importance of praying for her husband, knowing that he needs strength and endurance to face life's challenges. He loves that you cover him in prayer, cherishing a woman who seeks blessings and well-being for him and others. Even when you disagree with his decisions or actions, you find the courage to pray for him, asking God to guide him and lead him to the truth. That's the life of a powerful wife.

Wives, remember that prayer can save your marriage and transform both you and your husband. I had to learn to pray for my husband daily. Life is hard for men, and they often face immense pressure. But when you pray for him, you invite God to step in, provide help, and work things out. You don't need to fuss or get angry when he disappoints you. Just pray for him, and watch God change things, even convicting him to apologize and make amends.

When you realize that your husband belongs to God and that God is his head, you will find yourself praying for him more often.
You don't always need to voice your opinion or argue. Instead, tell God about it, and He will handle it. Your prayers invite God into your circumstances, and it gives him charge to take over your situations. Allow God to be the third strand that holds your marriage together. When God is the center of our marriage, we are stronger when God is invited in our marriage.

So, remember to pray for your husband before he leaves the house in the morning and at bedtime even throughout the day. Let him hear you praying for him; this will encourage him to work hard and complete his tasks. Make time to pray together, and watch God bless your marriage abundantly. Prayer is your weapon and your answer—use it!

Don't stop praying for your husband; he loves it when you pray for him.

Heavenly Father, thank you for teaching me to pray for my husband. He needs encouragement and your guidance. Show him the way and grant him favor in everything he does. In Jesus Name, Amen.

Psalm 91:11 NIV

For He will command his angels concerning you to guard you in all your ways

DAY 17 Don't Judge Him

Your husband appreciates that you don't judge him. He knows he doesn't always make the best decisions, and he makes mistakes and forgets things sometimes. And that's okay! Don't be hard on your man. I had to learn this myself. I was so hard on my husband because I knew he could do better, but he didn't need me to be his critic. He needed my encouragement and support. Don't be quick to judge his mistakes—none of us is perfect. He's human. He needs his wife, especially in tough times or when he messes up. Be there for him and remind him it's okay and that things will get better.

Remember, he's not Superman. He gets tired and doesn't have all the answers, but he tries every day to do his best. Sometimes things don't work out, and that's normal. Give him space to make errors and be supportive. He already feels bad when he messes up; don't add insult to injury. Instead, offer comfort and forgiveness. Your husband needs kindness and understanding, not anger and bitterness. When he makes a mistake, be quick to forgive him and move on. Just as you wouldn't want to hear judgment when you mess up, he doesn't either. He wants to hear encouragement.

So, remember, everyone makes mistakes. Have a forgiving response instead of a judgmental one. Next time your husband makes a mistake, encourage him and let him know it's okay. Be quick to forgive and move forward. Don't be the judge he doesn't need—be the wife he does.

Heavenly Father, help me to be mindful of not judging my husband's mistakes but to be quick to forgive him. None of us is perfect. Help me remember that and be an encouragement to him. In Jesus' name, Amen!

Ephesians 4:29 NLT

Don't use foul or abusive language. Let everything you say be good and helpful, so that your words will be an encouragement to those who hear them."

DAY 18 He likes That I'm his Safe Place

Your husband should trust you with his heart. You should be that person he turns to when he needs to release his anxiety and hurt. Men have feelings too, and they need a safe place to break down. Can he trust you with his pain and his reality, without fear of judgment? Your husband needs you to be there for him emotionally. Be loving and considerate of his feelings. Sometimes, hold your husband in your arms. I know you're used to him holding you, but your husband needs to feel secure and safe as well.

Imagine how wonderful it is for your husband to feel safe and trust you with his emotions. Men's hearts are tender, even if they hide it behind a tough exterior. Often, we as wives don't know when they are struggling internally because they put on a strong front. My husband once told me, "Sometimes I just need a hug." We as wives often expect them to give and give, but the reality is they need support too. After a long day at work, make sure you're ready to receive him when he comes home. Your home is his sanctuary, his wife is his safe and hiding place. Solomon says it like this:

"Your breasts are perfect;

they are twin deer

feeding among lilies.

[6] I will hasten to those hills

sprinkled with sweet perfume

He Likes All Of This

and stay there till sunrise. [7] My darling, you are lovely in every way. [8] My bride, together we will leave Lebanon! We will say goodbye to the peaks of Mount Amana, Senir, and Hermon, where lions and leopards live in the caves. [9] My bride, my very own, you have stolen my heart! With one glance from your eyes and the glow of your necklace, you have stolen my heart.

[10] Your love is sweeter than wine; the smell of your perfume is more fragrant than spices. [11] Your lips are a honeycomb; milk and honey flow from your tongue. Your dress has the aroma of cedar trees from Lebanon.

[12] My bride, my very own, you are a garden, a fountain closed off to all others. [13] Your

arms[h] are vines, covered with delicious fruits and all sorts of spices— henna, nard, [14] saffron, calamus, cinnamon, frankincense, myrrh, and aloes —all the finest spices. [15] You are a spring in the garden, a fountain of pure water, and a refreshing stream from Mount Lebanon."

Song of Solomon 4:5-15 CEV

So today, ladies, be sensitive to your husband's emotions and his hurt. Be that safe place where he can break down and let it all out. Be his confidant when he is weak, his strength that helps him put himself back together. Be his resting place. Your husband should feel restful with you and in you. Let him rest on you. So many times, my husband has fallen asleep on me because I am his resting place. Know that every day isn't a good day for him, but it can be better when he sees you.

Heavenly Father, help me to be my husband's safe place where he can confide. I know he will always look to you for guidance and safety. Help me to welcome him every day when he comes home and teach me how to build him up daily. In Jesus' name, Amen!

Proverbs 18:10 KJV

The name of the Lord is a strong tower: the righteous runneth into it and is safe.

DAY 19 Communication is Everything

Effective communication is the cornerstone of a successful marriage. Without it, you're likely facing challenges and misunderstandings. Proper communication is essential for resolving issues and ensuring both partners feel heard. It's impossible to solve problems if no one is truly listening. Being slow to speak and eager to listen is key. Listening to each other heart will produce positive solutions.

Healthy communication produces better solutions and outcomes. Developing these skills takes time. Our natural instinct is to respond defensively, but that's not effective communication. Instead, we should listen to understand why our spouse feels the way they do. Learning how to communicate healthily aiming to understand each other.

During heated conversations, someone needs to be mature enough to listen fully before reacting or getting angry. Timing is crucial—communicate at the right time to avoid escalating arguments. Remind each other, "healthy communication," when things get heated. It's best to relax and calm down before addressing concerns. While some situations require immediate attention, always strive to hear each other out. Many marriages struggle because couples can't or won't communicate properly. Refuse to yell or scream at each other. The goal is a healthy conversation that leads to solutions.

Today, talk to your husband and truly listen to his response. Don't be quick to get mad or judge. Speak in a way that lets him hear your heart. As you practice listening and understanding, the most important part of your marriage—communication—will heal. This is vital for your marriage to function with love and understanding. Be ready to understand each other and express your feelings in a heartfelt way. What comes from the heart reaches the heart. The more you practice this, the calmer and more peaceful your marriage will become.

Heavenly Father, thank you for giving us the tools to have healthy communication. Thank you for teaching us how to listen to each other's hearts and to have an ear to understand. Thank you, Father, for working out every situation we face. In Jesus' name, Amen!

Matthew 11:15

Anyone with ears to hear should listen and understand! **(NLT)**

He that hath ears to hear, let him hear. **(KJV)**

Chiquita N. Turner

DAY 20 Unity: Us Against the World

A power couple is a unified couple. When you said, "I do," you committed to becoming one. This oneness gives you the strength to stand against anything life throws at you. It's the most valuable lesson you can demonstrate and pass on to your children. While you are individuals, you are uniquely bonded to make significant impacts in this world. Supporting each other's dreams and careers is crucial in a marriage. We don't know what the future holds, but God does. Staying unified allows you to conquer and achieve whatever comes next.

Never be jealous or resentful of the favor God has placed on your spouse's life. Celebrate each other's victories and encourage each other to aim higher and do their best. Remember, your words of affirmation can motivate your man to Jump even when he feels unready. Always uplift each other, look out for one another, and demonstrate unity and togetherness. God commands a blessing when He sees unity. To keep those blessings in your marriage, stay unified and connected. You won't always agree, but you can always find common ground. Agree to disagree!

Work on your marriage together, include each other in decisions, and consider each other's feelings. You're not alone—you have a partner, a protector. Include him in your daily life. It's "Us against the World." Together, you can accomplish much, from raising your children to buying a house, investing in property, and establishing multiple streams of income. You can do all things through Christ who strengthens you. Your combined gifts and talents are meant to make a great impact in the world and in the lives of others.

Today, rekindle your unity and oneness by considering each other in your decisions. Communicate more about your dreams and goals. Encourage each other to fulfill those dreams. Create personal and family goal lists and set deadlines to achieve them. Remember, you are blessed when you are unified, and your husband has favor because he has you as his wife. The Bible says a man who finds a wife finds a good thing and obtains favor from God. Together, you have the perfect combination for success. Blessings and favor!

Heavenly Father, thank you for reminding me how to be blessed and to have favor in our lives. With You, we have everything we need, and You give us the ability to accomplish much in this world. Keep me and my husband unified in You. In Jesus' name, Amen!

Psalm 133:1 NIV

How good and pleasant it is when God's people live together in unity!

DAY 21 Your Enemy is the Devil, not Your Husband

Every marriage will face challenges, and there will be times when your spouse gets on your last nerve. You might not always like him, but you still love him. This is a natural part of marriage. When two people from different backgrounds come together, expect challenges. Differences in values, views, morals, disciplines, and perspectives can cause intense friction. Despite these difficulties, remember one thing: your husband is not your enemy; Satan is. When challenges arise, it's easy to fight or become defensive with your spouse. We might even attack them with our words and actions. As believers and Christian women, we must recognize when the adversary is at work in our marriage.

A prayer life is essential. Not every day will be sunshine and cake. There will be moments when you get tired and fed up, but your marriage is worth fighting for. Satan's job is to kill, steal, and destroy, including your marriage. God loves unity, but Satan seeks to bring division. Know that he is always working to destroy your life, joy, and happiness. He cannot stand to see you and your husband together. Many trials and tests will come in your marriage to challenge your faithfulness to God and your husband. Don't let him win!

Make an effort to pray more with your husband. Let your children hear you pray and saturate your home in prayer. Invite God into your situations and depend on Him to fix the problems. Prayer is a powerful weapon that God has given us; use it daily! God has also given us the power to defeat the devil and his devices. Whatever you don't like about your spouse, pray about it. Whatever you wish your husband would do more or less of, pray about it. Tell the Father, the one who made both of you. It's imperative that we don't fight each other but learn to recognize Satan's activities in our lives.

The devil is God's enemy, therefore he's your enemy. Never call your husband the devil but call out the spirit that might be operating in him. The devil can use anybody; no one is exempt from his attacks. Even you can be used by the devil if you're not fully aware of his activities. You might suddenly have a bad attitude for no reason or become frustrated with everything your husband does. The devil comes in many ways to throw you off your love and kindness. If you're not aware, you'll find yourself miserable for no apparent reason because Satan has tricked you into acting in a rude and bitter way.

Don't hold on to grudges—let them go! If your spouse has hurt you, tell him, and then ask God to heal your pain and heart. Satan's job is to constantly remind you of the hurt and pain you've suffered. He will constantly show you the bad and negative in your husband. Be aware that this is Satan's device to launch an attack on your marriage. Forgive your husband and let it go. Grow from the experience and allow God to fix your husband. You can't do it; only God can. Give your husband grace as the Lord gives us grace daily. Remove the shackles from him and free him in God's love again. Your husband really does love you!

So today, free yourself from past hurt and free your husband from the bondage of grudges or resentment with the help of the Lord.

Heavenly Father, lift the pain from my heart and heal me wherever I hurt. Open my eyes to see that Satan is my enemy, not my husband. Give me the power to overcome Satan's devices, so we are ready to defeat him when he comes. In Jesus' name, Amen!

2 Corinthians 2:11 KJV

Lest Satan should get an advantage over us: for we are not ignorant of his devices.

He Likes All Of This

DAY 22 Wife to Wife

I wrote this book to encourage you not to give up on your marriage. Difficult times and seasons will come, but learning to work through them is crucial. Your husband loves everything about you, though he may sometimes get distracted and forget to show it. Keep negative influences out of your ear and your marriage. Communication is key—talk to your man, don't yell or fuss. Sit down with him and express your concerns calmly. I have learned and now advocate for healthy communication. I refuse to yell and scream; those days are behind me. We are two adults who love each other and should be close enough to express our thoughts openly.

Keep intimacy at the core of your marriage. Intimacy isn't just sex; it's paying attention to each other, complimenting, encouraging, and cheering each other on. It's making time for each other. Intimacy is the heartbeat of a marriage. Don't stop touching and making each other feel special. Remember, your husband is your best friend and your man.

Treat him like your man, not like your son or a little boy. Respect him and follow his lead. Support him in his endeavors— you are his biggest cheerleader. Remember, what you won't do, someone else is ready and willing to. This isn't a threat but a reminder to stay vigilant and maintain your relationship. Don't get too comfortable—remain vigilant, spontaneous, and fun. Never withhold sex from your husband, he needs sex, and he chose you because he loves you and only wants sex from you. Remember what I said, "Overfeed Him" with your goodness! Make sure no doors are left open for the devil.

He Likes All Of This

I'm excited for you—it's never too late to begin again. Don't be afraid to seek counseling if needed; sometimes a mediator can help you work through issues. I recommend finding a Christian counselor for godly advice. Be better, not bitter. A happy wife leads to a happy life. Let your creative juices flow and be spontaneous.

I challenge you today to write down twenty-one affirmations to encourage your husband. Send him one of your personalized affirmations daily. Each month, be intentionally attentive to your man. Stay united, love him, and do good to him, and watch God bless your marriage. There is power in the number twenty-one— make good habits, say good things, because you are his good thing.

Heavenly Father, thank you for helping us become better wives. Thank you for giving us ways to improve our marriages and to build up our husbands. Teach our husbands to love us unconditionally, as the Bible commands. It is your will that we be one—help us achieve unity. During difficult times, remind us to stay calm and pray. Strengthen the wives today and help them accomplish all their goals. Give us creative ideas that will draw our families closer to you and to each other. Let love rule and abide in our homes forever. In Jesus' name, Amen!

Proverbs 18:22 ESV

He who finds a wife finds a good thing and obtains favor from the LORD.

Special Acknowledgements

I thank God for giving me insight to write this book.

Special thanks to my husband Anthony, and our amazing children AJ, Chiquirra, Diajah, Micaia, and Jonathan who has always supported me. I Love my Family!

To my dear friends and big sisters in Christ, Rolanda Holman and LaKesha Ford Calhoun, who encouraged me to write the book. Both of you have played an inspirational role in my life, pushing me to pursue the ideas God has given me. I love you both.

To my mother, Wanda G. M. Haymon, for always praying for me, encouraging me, and listening to me. You are my personal prayer warrior. Thank you for covering me daily in prayer. Thank you, Mama! I love you!

To the most powerful prayer team ever, "The Intercessors Prayer Line," thank you all for praying for me. Your prayers have carried me through the toughest days of my life. I love each one of you on the 5 AM and 12 Noon lines.

To my sweet, praying grandmother, "Big Mama," who has always given me wise advice on being a wife. Your leadership and love are with me always. I will never forget your words: "Nicole, be sweet to him, no matter what." I understand that now! Love you, Big Mama.

To my BEST friend who's always there for me, words can't express the impact you have made in my life spiritually, your encouragement has pushed me further than I could imagine. I Love You! Thank you!

To my beautiful married nieces, Kierra Cason and Ashley Vasquez, I am so proud of the women you have become, now wives and mothers. Thank you for being an example to my girls and your sisters. TeTe loves you both!

Your 21 Affirmation for your husband goes here….

Your Love letter to your husband goes here…

Your Love letter to your husband goes here…

Your Love letter to your husband goes here…

Your Love letter to your husband goes here…

Your Love letter to your husband goes here…

Your letter of concerns goes here…

Your letter of concerns goes here…

Your letter of concerns goes here…

Your letter of concerns goes here…

Your letter of concerns goes here…

Your date nights dates go here... Be Intentional! Set the Date!

21 prayers for your husband

Pray for your husband today…

Pray for your husband today…

Pray for your husband today…

Pray for your husband today…

Pray for your husband today…

Pray for your husband today…

Pray for your husband today…

Pray for your husband today...

Pray for your husband today…

Pray for your husband today…

Pray for your husband today…

Pray for your husband today…

Pray for your husband today…

Pray for your husband today…

Pray for your husband today…

Pray for your husband today…

Pray for your husband today…

Pray for your husband today…

Pray for your husband today…

Pray for your husband today…

Pray for your husband today…

Made in the USA
Columbia, SC
25 October 2024